Easy DIY Jewelry

BOOK 1

HIPPIE

ROCKER

GLAM

OCEAN

LEISURE ARTS, INC. • Little Rock, Arkansas

contents

8

6

41

28

1 HIPPIE | 4

2 OCEAN | 26

EDITORIAL STAFF
Vice President of Editorial: Susan White Sullivan
Special Projects Director: Susan Frantz Wiles
Director of E-Commerce and Prepress Services: Mark Hawkins
Creative Art Director: Katherine Laughlin
Technical Writers: Mary Sullivan Hutcheson, Frances Huddleston
Lisa Lancaster, and Jean Lewis
Special Projects Designer: Patti Wallenfang

Art Category Manager: Lora Puls
Graphic Artists: Kara Darling and Stacy Owens
Imaging Technician: Stephanie Johnson
Prepress Technician: Janie Marie Wright
Contributing Photographer: Ken West
Contributing Photo Stylists: Sondra Daniel and Christi Myers
Manager of E-Commerce: Robert Young

64

65

78

72

3 GLAM | 46

4 ROCKER | 68

BUSINESS STAFF
President and Chief Executive Officer: Rick Barton
Vice President of Finance: Laticia Mull Dittrich
Director of Corporate Planning: Anne Martin
National Sales Director: Martha Adams
Information Technology Director: Brian Roden
Controller: Francis Caple
Vice President of Operations: Jim Dittrich
Retail Customer Service Manager: Stan Raynor
Vice President of Purchasing: Fred F. Pruss

We have made every effort to ensure that these instructions are accurate and complete. We cannot, however, be responsible for human error, typographical mistakes, or variations in individual work.

Library of Congress Control Number: 2013931599
ISBN-13: 978-1-4647-1173-2

CHAPTER ONE

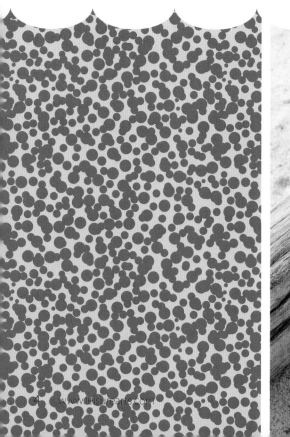

hippie

Get back to nature with necklaces, earrings, and bracelets you made yourself! Today's fun beads and jewelry accents include the look of leather, wood, and semi-precious stones. Colorful cords and jute also add earthy beauty to these timeless fashions. Beginning on page 90, you'll learn all about the supplies, tools, and easy techniques that shape these peaceful creations.

CHANDELIER EARRINGS

You'll need:

◆ 2 silver filigree teardrop shapes
◆ 8 small turquoise beads
◆ 8 amber bugle beads
◆ 8 small bronze beads
◆ 8 small silver beads
◆ 2 silver ear wires with attached pinch bails
◆ 8 silver headpins
◆ 8 silver jump rings
◆ chain-nose pliers, round-nose pliers, and wire cutters

Read Jewelry Making Basics, pages 90-96, before making your earrings.

For each earring:

1. Make 4 bead dangles *(page 95)* with beads and head pins.
2. Use the jump rings *(page 95)* to attach the dangles to the teardrop.
3. Attach the teardrop to the ear wire pinch bail *(Fig. 1)*.

Fig. 1

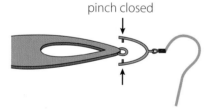

pinch closed

FLOWER & CHAIN NECKLACES

Flower necklace approx. length: 32", excluding pendant
Chain necklace approx. length: 53"

You'll need:
◆ copper metal flower pendant
◆ large orange glass butterfly bead
◆ assorted medium and small metal and glass beads (we used 7)
◆ 35" length orange suede cord
◆ decorative silver oval
◆ antique copper chain
◆ antique copper large oval jump ring
◆ antique copper large round jump rings
◆ antique copper head pin
◆ antique copper eye pin
◆ chain-nose pliers, round-nose pliers, and wire cutters

Read Jewelry Making Basics, pages 90-96, before making your necklaces.

To make the necklaces:
1. For the chain necklace, use the oval jump ring *(page 95)* to join the ends of a 52" chain length.
2. For the flower necklace, fold the suede cord length in half and loop through the silver oval *(Photo 1)*. Knot the ends together.

Photo 1

3. Twisting the ends together at the pendant back, use an eye pin to attach a bead to the flower center.
4. Make a bead dangle *(page 95)* using the butterfly bead, the remaining beads, and a head pin. Use the round jump rings to attach the dangle to the pendant and the pendant to the silver oval.

NATURAL BRACELETS

Stretchy Bracelet
You'll need:
- large stone beads (we used 6)
- assorted medium and small wood beads (we used 24)
- stretch cord
- silver jump rings
- silver head pins
- jeweler's glue
- chain-nose pliers, round-nose pliers, and wire cutters
- flexible wire beading needle (optional)

Read Jewelry Making Basics, pages 90-96, before making your bracelet.

To make the Stretchy Bracelet:
1. With a bead stop at one end **(Fig. 1)**, thread the wood beads on a 12" length of cord.

Fig. 1

2. Check the bracelet size, adding or removing beads until the bracelet is the right length. Remove the bead stop. Tie the cord with a surgeon's knot **(Fig. 2)** and apply a drop of glue to the knot. Once dry, trim the cord ends.

Fig. 2

3. Make 6 bead dangles *(page 95)* using the stone beads and head pins.
4. Use the jump rings *(page 95)* to attach the dangles to the bracelet.

Leather Bracelet
You'll need:
- pre-made leather bracelet
- silver tree pendant
- assorted large, medium, and small beads (we used 5)
- 2 silver charms
- silver bail
- silver jump rings
- silver head pin
- chain-nose pliers, round-nose pliers, and wire cutters

Read Jewelry Making Basics, pages 90-96, before making your bracelet.

To make the Leather Bracelet:
1. Make a bead dangle *(page 95)* using the beads and head pin.
2. Use the jump rings *(page 95)* to attach the bead dangle, charms, and pendant to the bail.
3. Thread the bail on the bracelet.

Chunky Bracelet
You'll need:
- ◆ large stone beads (we used 5)
- ◆ large wood beads (we used 4)
- ◆ small crystal beads (we used 12)
- ◆ silver toggle clasp
- ◆ silver nylon-coated beading wire
- ◆ silver crimp beads and crimp tool
- ◆ wire cutters

Read Jewelry Making Basics, pages 90-96, before making your bracelet.

To make the Chunky Bracelet:
1. Use a crimp bead *(page 96)* to attach 1 clasp end to a 14" wire length.
2. Thread the beads on the wire. Check the bracelet size, adding or removing beads until the bracelet is the right length. Be sure to use some smaller beads near the clasp bar so you can fit the bar through the clasp loop.
3. Use a crimp bead to attach the remaining clasp end to the bracelet.

CAREFREE NECKLACES

Chain Necklace

Chain necklace approx. length: 20", excluding pendant

You'll need:
- turquoise pendant with attached charms and bail **(Photo 1)**
- 8 medium amber oval beads
- assorted medium and small metal and glass beads (we used 7)
- antique copper chain
- antique copper toggle clasp
- antique copper jump rings
- antique copper head pin
- antique copper eye pins
- chain-nose pliers, round-nose pliers, and wire cutters

Photo 1

Read Jewelry Making Basics, pages 90-96, before making your necklace.

To make the Chain Necklace:
1. Remove the bead dangle that came attached to the pendant. Make a long bead dangle *(page 95)* using the assorted beads and a head pin. Use a jump ring *(page 95)* to attach the bead dangle to the pendant.
2. To make the beaded connector, thread a bead on an eye pin. Make a loop at the wire end **(Photo 2)**. Make 8 connectors.

Photo 2

3. For the necklace, cut the chain into one 3¹/₂", two 2", and six 1¹/₈" lengths.
4. Thread the pendant on the 3¹/₂" chain length and attach a connector to each chain end.
5. Alternating the chain lengths and the connectors, attach three 1¹/₈" chain lengths and 3 connectors to one end of the necklace. Finish off with a 2" chain length and a clasp end.
6. Repeat Step 5 on the other side of the necklace.

Beaded Necklace

Beaded necklace approx. length: 26", excluding pendant

You'll need:
- metal crescent moon pendant with attached star charm
- assorted small round glass beads (we used 140)
- large silver jump ring
- beading thread
- beading needle
- jeweler's glue

Read Jewelry Making Basics, pages 90-96, before making your necklace.

Continued on page 12.

To make the Beaded Necklace:
1. With a bead stop at one end **(Fig. 1)**, use the beading needle to thread the beads on a 38" beading thread length, until the beaded section is 26" long.

Fig. 1

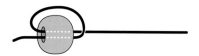

2. Remove the bead stop. Tie thread with a surgeon's knot **(Fig. 2)** and apply a drop of glue to the knot. Once dry, trim the thread ends.

Fig. 2

3. Attach the pendant to the necklace with the jump ring *(page 95)*.

Pendant Necklace
Pendant necklace approx. length: 16", excluding pendant

You'll need:
◆ turquoise/silver pendant with attached bail
◆ pre-made braided leather necklace

Read Jewelry Making Basics, pages 90-96, before making your necklace.

To make the Pendant Necklace:
For a quick and easy necklace, thread a large pendant on a pre-made necklace.

COLORFUL BRACELETS

Suede Bracelet
You'll need:
◆ 3 large red ceramic beads
◆ 2 medium silver beads
◆ two 14" lengths tan suede cord
◆ two 12" lengths dark tan jute cord
◆ silver toggle clasp
◆ 2 large silver oval jump rings
◆ jeweler's glue
◆ chain-nose pliers

Read Jewelry Making Basics, pages 90-96, before making your bracelet.

To make the Suede Bracelet:
1. Thread the beads on the suede cord lengths. Centering the beads, tie overhand knots *(page 96)* to hold the beads in place.
2. Attach a jump ring *(page 95)* to each toggle clasp piece.
3. Determine how long you want the finished bracelet. Subtract the clasp length and the length of the beaded/knotted area. Divide this by 2.
4. Adding 1¹/₂" for a tail, trim each suede cord to the measurement determined in Step 3.
5. Thread the suede cords at one end through a jump ring and fold over *(Fig. 1)*.

Fig. 1

6. Form a loop with a dark tan jute length. Wrap the jute around the folded suede 4-5 times. Bring the end through the loop *(Fig. 2)*. Pull firmly on the opposite end of the jute until the loop disappears.

Fig. 2

7. Place a drop of glue on the top and bottom jute ends. When the glue is dry, trim the jute ends *(Fig. 3)*.

Fig. 3

8. Repeat Steps 5-7 on the opposite end to complete the bracelet. For the fringed ends, make 1" long cuts in each suede cord tail.

Stretchy Bracelet
You'll need:
◆ assorted beads (we used 30)
◆ stretch cord
◆ jeweler's glue
◆ flexible wire beading needle (optional)

Read Jewelry Making Basics, pages 90-96, before making your bracelet.

Continued on page 14

To make the Stretchy Bracelet:

1. With a bead stop at one end *(Fig. 4)*, thread beads on a 12" length of cord.

Fig. 4

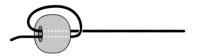

2. Check the bracelet size, adding or removing beads until the bracelet is the right length. Remove the bead stop. Tie the cord with a surgeon's knot *(Fig. 5)* and apply a drop of glue to the knot. Once dry, trim the cord ends.

Fig. 5

Chain Bracelet
You'll need:
- large square flat bead
- assorted medium and small wood, glass, and metal beads and spacers (we used 14)
- antique copper chain
- antique copper toggle clasp
- antique copper nylon-coated beading wire
- antique copper jump rings
- antique copper crimp beads and crimp tool
- chain-nose pliers and wire cutters

Read Jewelry Making Basics, pages 90-96, before making your bracelet.

To make the Chain Bracelet:

1. Use a crimp bead *(page 96)* to attach a 9" wire length to a jump ring.
2. Thread the beads and spacers on the wire until the beaded area measures about 4$^1/_2$". Use a crimp bead to attach another jump ring.
3. Determine how long you want the finished bracelet. Subtract the clasp length and the length of the beaded segment. Cut a length of chain this long. Cut it in half.
4. Attach the beaded segment *(page 95)* to the chain ends. Use jump rings to attach the clasp to the chain ends.

JUTE NECKLACES

Approx. length: 15"-16"

For the Cream Necklace, you'll need:
◆ teardrop pendant
◆ assorted large, medium, and small square and tube wood beads (we used 13)
◆ large flat round wood bead for clasp
◆ four 60" lengths cream jute cord
◆ antique copper jump ring
◆ chain-nose pliers

For the Brown Necklace, you'll need:
◆ medium orange glass beads (we used 6)
◆ medium brown/orange wood beads (we used 7)
◆ large flat round wood bead for clasp
◆ two 120" lengths brown jute cord

Read Jewelry Making Basics, pages 90-96, before making your necklaces.

To make the Cream Necklace:
1. Holding the 4 lengths together, knot the cords 1", 2", and 4$^1/_2$" from one end with overhand knots *(page 96)*. Thread a square bead on the two middle cords.
2. Tie 3 square knots **(Fig. 1)**. Thread a tube bead on the two middle cords. Tie 3 square knots.

Fig. 1

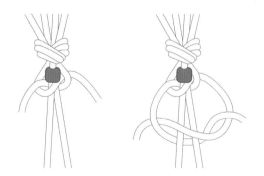

3. Knotting once between beads, thread 3 small square beads on the middle cords **(Photo 1)**. Tie 3 square knots.

Photo 1

4. Thread a tube bead on the two middle cords; tie 3 square knots. Thread a square bead on the middle two cords.
5. Repeat Steps 2-4. Knot the cords close to the last bead with an overhand knot, skip 2" and knot the cords again.
6. Tie a knot around the flat round bead with two cords. Trim the cord ends.
7. Attach the pendant to the necklace with the jump ring *(page 95)*.

To make the Brown Necklace:
1. Holding both ends together, fold the cord lengths in half. Tie an overhand knot *(page 96)* 1" from the fold.
2. Tie 5 square knots **(Fig. 1)**.
3. Thread a wood bead on the middle 2 cords **(Photo 2)**. Tie 5 square knots. Thread a glass bead on the middle 2 cords.

Photo 2

4. Repeat Steps 2-3 until the necklace measures 16". Tie an overhand knot ½" from the last square knot.
5. Thread the flat round bead on the cords and tie an overhand knot. Trim the cord ends.

FLOWER EARRINGS

You'll need:

- ◆ 2 large wood flower medallions
- ◆ 2 medium red flat disc beads
- ◆ 2 small silver beads
- ◆ 4 small turquoise beads
- ◆ 2 silver eye pins
- ◆ 2 large silver jump rings
- ◆ 2 silver ear wires
- ◆ chain-nose pliers, round-nose pliers, and wire cutters

Read Jewelry Making Basics, pages 90-96, before making your earrings.

For each earring:

1. To make a beaded connector, thread the beads on an eye pin. Make a loop *(page 95)* at the wire end *(Photo 1)*.

Photo 1

2. Use a jump ring *(page 95)* to attach a medallion to the connector.
3. Attach the connector to the ear wire.

BIRDS ON A BRANCH NECKLACE

Approx. length: 18"

You'll need:

◆ silver metal branch pendant
◆ assorted medium and small metal, glass, and wood beads (we used 38)
◆ silver chain
◆ large silver jump rings
◆ silver toggle clasp
◆ silver nylon-coated beading wire
◆ silver crimp beads and crimp tool
◆ chain-nose pliers and wire cutters

Read Jewelry Making Basics, pages 90-96, before making your necklace.

To make the necklace:

1. Attach a jump ring *(page 95)* to a 3^1/$_2$" chain length. Attach a clasp end to the opposite end. Repeat using another 3^1/$_2$" chain length, jump ring, and the remaining clasp end.
2. Use a crimp bead *(page 96)* to attach an 8" wire length to one end of the pendant. Thread the beads on the wire until the beaded area measures about 4".
3. Thread the wire end through a chain jump ring, a crimp bead, and back through the first few threaded beads. Secure the crimp bead and trim the wire.
4. Repeat Steps 2-3 on the other side to complete the necklace.

TASSEL NECKLACE

Approx. length: 30", excluding tassel

You'll need:
- ◆ 36" length brown suede cord
- ◆ four 15" lengths brown waxed cord
- ◆ large wood ring
- ◆ large wood bead
- ◆ assorted charms (we used 4)
- ◆ assorted large, medium, and small metal, stone, glass, and wood beads (we used 13)
- ◆ silver peace sign link
- ◆ 2¹/₂" bronze chain length
- ◆ silver cord ends
- ◆ assorted silver, gold, and bronze head pins
- ◆ bronze eye pin
- ◆ assorted silver, gold, and bronze jump rings
- ◆ flat-nose pliers, round-nose pliers, and wire cutters

Read Jewelry Making Basics, pages 90-96, before making your necklace.

To make the necklace:
1. Fold the suede cord in half and loop it through the wood ring **(Photo 1)**. Knot the ends together.

Photo 1

2. Holding the lengths together, thread the waxed cords through the wood bead, the wood ring, and back through the wood bead. Knot the cords together below the bead. Trim the cords to varying lengths.
3. To make the beaded connector, thread a bead on the eye pin. Make a loop *(page 95)* at the wire end **(Photo 2)**.

Photo 2

4. Make 6 bead dangles *(page 95)* using the assorted beads and head pins.
5. Placing as desired along the cord lengths and on the ends, use the cord ends and jump rings *(page 95)* to attach the charms, chain length, silver link, beaded connector, and bead dangles to the cords.

PEACE SIGN EARRINGS

You'll need:
- 2 very large silver metal peace sign pendants
- 2 medium orange flat glass beads
- 2 medium metal butterfly beads
- 12 assorted medium and small metal, glass, and wood beads (in pairs)
- 2 metal leaf charms
- turquoise linked beads chain
- 2 silver ear wires
- silver head pins
- silver eye pins
- silver jump rings
- chain-nose pliers, round-nose pliers, and wire cutters

Read Jewelry Making Basics, pages 90-96, before making your earrings.

For each earring:
1. For the leaf dangle, make a beaded connector by threading beads on an eye pin. Make a loop *(page 95)* at the wire end **(Photo 1)**. Attach a leaf charm to one end of the connector *(page 95)*.

Photo 1

2. For the butterfly dangle, make a beaded connector by threading beads on an eye pin. Make a loop at the wire end **(Photo 2)**. Make a bead dangle *(page 95)* with a butterfly bead and a head pin. Attach the dangle to one end of the connector.

Photo 2

Fig. 1

3. Attach the pendant to the ear wire.
4. Fold a 6¹/₂" chain length in half and attach to a jump ring *(Fig. 1)*.

5. Attach the leaf and butterfly dangles to the jump ring.
6. Attach the jump ring to the pendant.

MEDALLION BRACELET

You'll need:
- gold filigree medallion
- 6 assorted medium green glass beads
- 2 small metal spacer beads
- one 12" and four 40" lengths green cord
- jeweler's glue

Read Jewelry Making Basics, pages 90-96, before making your bracelet.

To make the bracelet:
1. To make 1 side of the bracelet, fold 2 long cord lengths in half and loop through the medallion *(Photo 1)*. Tie a square knot *(Fig. 1)*.

Photo 1

Fig. 1

2. Thread a bead on the two middle cords. Tie 2 square knots. Repeat twice or until side measures about 2" from the medallion.
3. Thread on a spacer and tie 3 square knots. Add more or less knots to lengthen or shorten your bracelet length as needed.
4. Tie an overhand knot *(page 96)* ¹/₂" from the last square knot. Trim the cord ends.
5. For the opposite side, repeat Steps 1-3.
6. Fold the bracelet cord ends over to make a loop. Form a loop with the 12" cord length. Wrap the cord length around the bracelet cord 4-5 times. Bring the end through the loop *(Fig. 2)*. Pull firmly on the opposite end until the cord end disappears.

Fig. 2

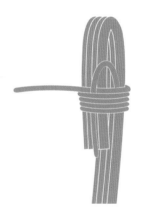

7. Place a drop of glue on the top and bottom cord ends. When the glue is dry, trim the cord ends *(Fig. 3)*.

Fig. 3

CHAPTER TWO

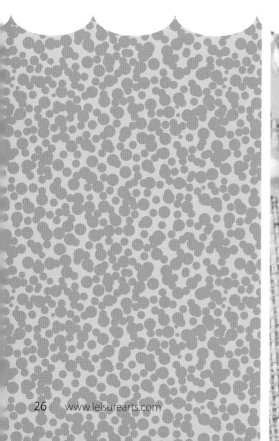

ocean

It's so easy to fashion your own rare treasures from the sea!
Wear an armful of aquatic-themed bracelets. Add bead
earrings that remind you of polished sea glass. And adorn
yourself with necklaces in the hues of a peaceful lagoon.

BEAD DANGLE EARRINGS

You'll need:

- 16 assorted large, medium, and small blue and white beads (in pairs)
- 2 silver jump rings
- 8 silver head pins
- 2 large silver kidney ear wires
- chain-nose pliers, round-nose pliers, and wire cutters

Read Jewelry Making Basics, pages 90-96, before making your earrings.

For each earring:

1. Make a large bead dangle *(page 95)* with a large bead, using a smaller bead at the bottom.
2. Make 3 smaller bead dangles with the beads and head pins. Attach to a jump ring *(page 95)* to form a dangle cluster.
3. Slide the dangle cluster and large bead dangle on an ear wire.

CHARM BRACELET

You'll need:

- 5 assorted silver charms
- assorted medium and small silver, faux pearl, aqua, and green beads
- silver jump rings
- silver head pins
- silver chain bracelet
- chain-nose pliers, round-nose pliers, and wire cutters

Read Jewelry Making Basics, pages 90-96, before making your bracelet.

To make the bracelet:

1. Make 8 bead dangles *(page 95)*, using a head pin and 3-4 beads per dangle.
2. Attach each dangle to the bracelet *(page 95)*.
3. Use a jump ring to attach each charm to the bracelet.

CHARM EARRINGS

You'll need:

- 4 silver seashell charms (in pairs)
- 6 small green and blue beads (in pairs)
- 2 small and 4 large silver jump rings
- 6 silver head pins
- 2 silver ear wires
- chain-nose pliers, round-nose pliers, and wire cutters

Read Jewelry Making Basics, pages 90-96, before making your earrings.

For each earring:

1. Make 3 bead dangles *(page 95)* with the beads and head pins. Attach to a small jump ring *(page 95)*, making a dangle cluster.
2. Use a large jump ring to attach the dangle cluster and a charm to an ear wire. Use another large jump ring to attach a second charm to the ear wire.

CHUNKY BEAD BRACELET

You'll need:

- ◆ large green acrylic beads (we used 7)
- ◆ medium green acrylic beads (we used 4)
- ◆ silver toggle clasp with attached
     heart charm
- ◆ silver nylon-coated beading wire
- ◆ silver crimp beads and crimp tool
- ◆ wire cutters

Read Jewelry Making Basics, pages 90-96,
before making your bracelet.

To make the bracelet:

1. Use a crimp bead *(page 96)* to
   attach one end of the clasp to
   a 14" wire length.
2. Beginning and ending with the
   medium beads, thread the beads
   on the wire. Check the bracelet
   size, adding or removing beads
   until the bracelet is the right
   length.
3. Use a crimp bead to attach
   the remaining clasp end to the
   bracelet.

TIP: If you choose a toggle without a charm,
one can easily be added with a jump ring.

CHOKER

You'll need:
- wire choker with a removable magnetic clasp
- assorted medium and small beads, charms, and shells
- 2 silver cones
- silver eye pins
- silver jump rings
- chain-nose pliers, round-nose pliers, and wire cutters

Read Jewelry Making Basics, pages 90-96, before making your choker.

To make the choker:
1. To make the beaded connector, thread beads and shells on an eye pin. Make a loop *(page 95)* at the wire end *(Photo 1)*. Make 3 beaded connectors. Use jump rings *(page 95)* to attach a charm to each connector.

2. Attach jump rings to two shells.
3. Unscrew the clasp from the choker. Thread a cone on the choker wire. Then add beads, beaded connectors, and shells as desired. End with the remaining cone and replace the clasp.

Photo 1

CRAB PENDANT NECKLACE

Approx. length: 16", excluding pendant

You'll need:
- ◆ small seed beads (about 230)
- ◆ 22 medium glass beads
- ◆ crab and faux pearl pendant
- ◆ large silver jump ring
- ◆ silver toggle clasp
- ◆ silver nylon-coated beading wire
- ◆ silver crimp beads and crimp tool
- ◆ chain-nose pliers and wire cutters

Read Jewelry Making Basics, pages 90-96, before making your necklace.

To make the necklace:
1. Attach the jump ring *(page 95)* to the pendant.
2. Use a crimp bead *(page 96)* to attach one end of the clasp to a 28" wire length.
3. Beginning and ending with the small seed beads and adding the pendant at the center, thread the beads on the wire until the beaded section is 15" long. Use a crimp bead to attach the remaining clasp end to the necklace.

DANGLE NECKLACE

Approx. length: 32", excluding pendant

You'll need:
- ◆ aqua, green, and white cotton cord
- ◆ green ribbon
- ◆ assorted medium and small beads, shells, and charms
- ◆ shell ring
- ◆ shell fish pendant
- ◆ large silver jump ring
- ◆ chain-nose pliers

Read Jewelry Making Basics, pages 90-96, before making your necklace.

To make the necklace:
1. Cut a 40" length of each cord. Fold the cords in half and loop through the shell ring *(Fig. 1)*. Knot all the ends together.

Fig. 1

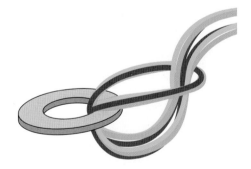

2. Tie an 8" aqua cord length to the shell ring. Thread on beads, charms, and shells as desired; knot and trim the ends.
3. Loop a 10" white cord length through the shell ring. Thread on beads and shells as desired, using the jump ring *(page 95)* to attach a shell. Knot and trim the ends.
4. Tie on the fish pendant with ribbon.

GLASS PENDANT NECKLACE

You'll need:
- ◆ glass pendant
- ◆ 2 large metal-lined glass beads
- ◆ 2 jeweled spacer beads
- ◆ pre-made cord/ribbon necklace

Read Jewelry Making Basics, pages 90-96, before making your necklace.

To make the necklace:
Thread the spacers, beads, and pendant on the necklace.

TIP: If the necklace clasp is a bit too wide to fit through the beads, use chain-nose pliers to gently open the clasp. Thread the beads on the necklace and replace the clasp.

LONG BEADED NECKLACE

Approx. length: 60"

You'll need:
- ◆ assorted medium and large beads in blue, aqua, green, and silver (we used 116)
- ◆ small silver beads (we used 117)
- ◆ beading thread
- ◆ beading needle
- ◆ jeweler's glue

Read Jewelry Making Basics, pages 90-96, before making your necklace.

To make the necklace:
1. With a bead stop at one end *(Fig. 1)*, thread the beads on a 72" thread length, placing a small silver bead between each assorted bead.

Fig. 1

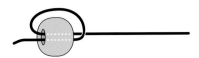

2. Remove the bead stop and tie the thread ends together in a surgeon's knot *(Fig. 2)*. Place a drop of jeweler's glue on the knot. When dry, trim the thread ends.

Fig. 2

RIBBON BRACELET

You'll need:
- 2 large metal-lined glass beads
- 5 silver spacer beads, one with a charm
- assorted ribbons
- silver clasp
- large silver jump rings
- chain-nose pliers

Read Jewelry Making Basics, pages 90-96, before making your bracelet.

To make the bracelet:
1. Thread the beads and spacers on the ribbons.
2. Tie one end of the ribbons to a jump ring. Check the bracelet length and tie the other end to a jump ring.
3. Attach the jump rings *(page 95)* to the clasp.

STRETCHY BRACELETS

For each bracelet, you'll need:
- assorted medium and small beads (we used about 33-60 per bracelet)
- stretch cord
- jeweler's glue
- flexible wire beading needle (optional)

You'll also need:
- ribbon

Read Jewelry Making Basics, pages 90-96, before making your bracelets.

To make each bracelet:
1. With a bead stop at one end, thread beads on a 12" length of cord *(Fig. 1)*.

Fig. 1

2. Check the bracelet size, adding or removing beads until the bracelet is the right length. Remove the bead stop and tie the cord with a surgeon's knot *(Fig. 2)* and apply a drop of glue to the knot. Once dry, trim the cord ends.

Fig. 2

3. Make 5 bracelets and tie together with a ribbon bow.

SUEDE NECKLACE

Approx. length: 38"

You'll need:
- ◆ two 45" lengths of aqua suede cord
- ◆ 25" length of small silver chain
- ◆ assorted seed beads
- ◆ 12 large and 6 medium blue crystal beads
- ◆ 2 large silver jump rings
- ◆ silver nylon-coated beading wire
- ◆ silver crimp beads and crimp tool
- ◆ chain-nose pliers and wire cutters

Read Jewelry Making Basics, pages 90-96, before making your necklace.

To make the necklace:
1. For the beaded segment, cut a 20" length of wire. Thread a seed bead on the wire and fold the wire in half. Holding the wire ends together, thread beads on the wire until the beaded section is 8" long. Use a crimp bead *(page 96)* to attach a jump ring to the end. Repeat to make another beaded segment.
2. Attach the jump rings *(page 95)* on the beaded segments to the chain ends.
3. Thread 2 large beads on each suede cord end. Knot the ends and trim.
4. Knot beaded suede and chain lengths together about 4" from the ends.

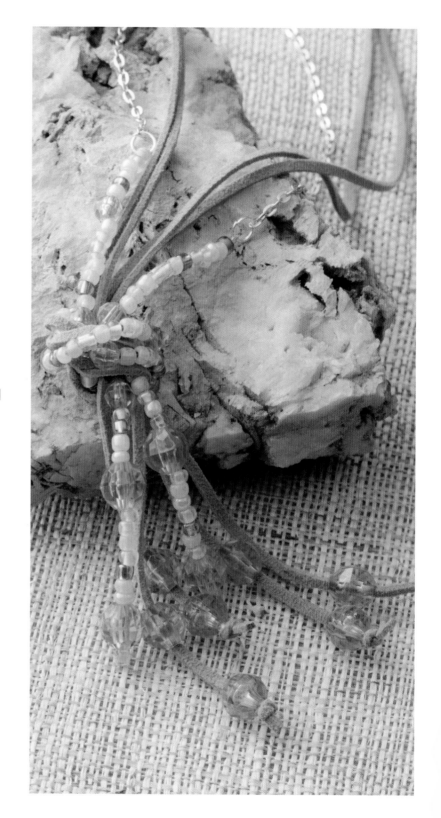

TWO-COLOR BEADED NECKLACE

Approx. length: 19", excluding pendant

You'll need:

- ◆ large seed beads in blue and green (about 80 each)
- ◆ 4 silver spacers
- ◆ silver starfish pendant
- ◆ large silver jump ring
- ◆ silver toggle clasp
- ◆ silver nylon-coated beading wire
- ◆ silver crimp beads and crimp tool
- ◆ chain-nose pliers and wire cutters

Read Jewelry Making Basics, pages 90-96, before making your necklace.

To make the necklace:

1. Use a crimp bead *(page 96)* to attach one end of the clasp to a 24" wire length.
2. Attach the jump ring *(page 95)* to the pendant.
3. Alternating bead colors, thread the beads, spacers, and pendant on the wire.
4. Use a crimp bead to attach the remaining clasp end to the necklace.

MULTI-STRAND BRACELET

You'll need:
- ◆ assorted medium and small beads in blue and silver (we used 82)
- ◆ 3 silver turtle links
- ◆ 2 silver cones
- ◆ silver lobster clasp
- ◆ silver eye pins and head pins
- ◆ silver jump rings
- ◆ silver nylon-coated beading wire
- ◆ silver crimp beads and crimp tool
- ◆ spring bead stop
- ◆ chain-nose pliers, round-nose pliers, and wire cutters

Read Jewelry Making Basics, pages 90-96, before making your bracelet.

For this bracelet, you'll need to decide the bracelet length ahead of time, taking into account the length of the silver cones and clasp. You may use more or less beads than shown on the connectors and near the clasp to get the right length.

To make the bracelet:

1. To make a beaded strand, thread beads on a 12" wire length to the determined bracelet length, using the spring bead stop as necessary; secure with a crimp bead *(page 96)* at each end. Repeat to make a second beaded strand *(Photo 1)*.

Photo 1

2. For the turtle strand, make 4 beaded connectors by threading 2-3 beads on an eye pin. Make a loop *(page 95)* at the wire end *(Photo 2)*. Join the connectors to the turtle links *(page 95)*.

3. Loop a 6" wire length through each end connector. Fold the wire in half and secure with a crimp bead *(Photo 3)*.

Photo 2

Photo 3

4. Thread the turtle and beaded strands through a cone and secure with a crimp bead. Trim two of the four wires *(Photo 4)*. Repeat for the other end with the remaining cone.

Photo 4

trim 2 wires

Photo 5

5. Thread 1-3 beads, a crimp bead, and the clasp on one end; thread the wire back through the crimp bead and the beads *(Photo 5)*. Secure the crimp bead and trim the wire ends. Repeat with a jump ring (instead of the clasp) on the opposite end.

6. Use a jump ring to add a bead dangle *(page 95)* near the clasp.

BEAD FRINGE EARRINGS

You'll need:

◆ 84 assorted clear, blue, and grey seed beads
◆ 2 silver bead caps
◆ 2 silver ear wires
◆ silver jump rings
◆ silver eye pins
◆ silver head pins
◆ silver nylon-coated beading wire
◆ silver crimp beads and crimp tool
◆ chain-nose pliers, round-nose pliers, and wire cutters

Read Jewelry Making Basics, pages 90-96, before making your earrings.

For each earring:

1. Make 6 bead dangles *(page 95)* with beads and head pins.
2. To make the beaded connector, thread 3 beads on an eye pin. Make a loop at the wire end *(Photo 1)*. Make 12 connectors.

Photo 1

3. Join 2 bead connectors *(page 95)* and a bead dangle *(Photo 2)*. Repeat to make 6 bead fringe pieces.

Photo 2

4. Attach 3 bead fringe pieces to a jump ring; repeat.

5. Thread both jump rings on a 6" wire length. Thread the wire ends through a bead cap, a crimp bead, an ear wire, and back through the crimp bead and bead cap *(Fig. 1)*. Secure the crimp bead *(page 96)* and trim the excess wire, being careful not to cut the beaded fringe.

Fig. 1

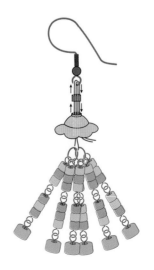

CHAPTER THREE

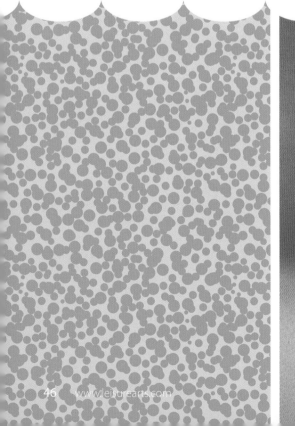

glam

Did you know? Stunning jewelry is easy to make! All the information you need for choosing beads and findings begins on page 90. You'll also learn all the basics on today's jewelry-making tools and techniques. It's truly simple to get more glamour in your life while adding sparkle to any occasion!

PEACOCK PENDANT NECKLACE

Approx. length: 26", excluding pendant

You'll need:

- antique gold peacock pendant
- assorted medium and small green and blue beads (we used 78)
- medium antique gold beads (we used 10)
- medium gold/rhinestone beads (we used 13)
- gold hook and eye clasp
- large gold jump ring
- gold nylon-coated beading wire
- gold crimp beads and crimp tool
- chain-nose pliers and wire cutters

Read Jewelry Making Basics, pages 90-96, before making your necklace.

To make the necklace:

1. Use a crimp bead *(page 96)* to attach a 30" wire length to one end of the clasp. Thread beads on the wire until the beaded section is 25" long. Use a crimp bead to attach the remaining clasp end to the necklace.
2. Use the jump ring *(page 95)* to attach the pendant to the necklace center.

CRYSTAL BRACELET SET

For the Toggle Clasp bracelet, you'll need:
- large clear acrylic beads (we used 7)
- silver/rhinestone beads (we used 8)
- silver beads (we used 6)
- silver nylon-coated beading wire
- silver crimp beads and crimp tool
- silver toggle clasp with heart charm
- wire cutters

For the Crystal Stretch bracelet, you'll need:
- assorted medium and small crystal and faux pearl beads (we used 24)
- stretch cord
- jeweler's glue
- flexible wire beading needle (optional)

Read Jewelry Making Basics, pages 90-96, before making your bracelets.

To make the Toggle Clasp bracelet:
1. Use a crimp bead *(page 96)* to attach one end of the clasp to a 12" wire length.
2. Thread the beads on the wire. Check the bracelet size, adding or removing beads until the bracelet is the right length. Be sure to use some smaller beads near the clasp bar so you can fit the bar through the clasp loop.
3. Use a crimp bead to attach the remaining clasp end to the bracelet.

To make the Crystal Stretch bracelet:
1. With a bead stop *(Fig. 1)* at one end, thread beads on a 12" length of cord.

Fig. 1

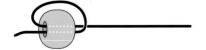

2. Check the bracelet size, adding or removing beads, until the bracelet is the right length. Remove the bead stop. Tie the cord with a surgeon's knot *(Fig. 2)* and apply a drop of glue to the knot. Once dry, trim the cord ends.

Fig. 2

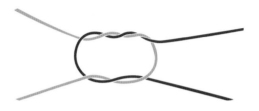

LEOPARD & CHAIN BRACELETS

For the Leopard Stretch Bracelet, you'll need:
◆ large leopard print flat round beads (we used 6)
◆ small gold/rhinestone beads (we used 6)
◆ stretch cord
◆ jeweler's glue
◆ flexible wire beading needle (optional)

For the Chain Bracelet, you'll need:
◆ assorted width gold chains
◆ large gold jump rings
◆ gold toggle clasp
◆ chain-nose pliers and wire cutters

Read Jewelry Making Basics, pages 90-96, before making your bracelets.

To make the Leopard Stretch Bracelet:
1. With a bead stop at one end *(Fig. 1)*, thread beads on a 12" length of cord.

Fig. 1

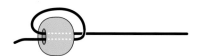

2. Check the bracelet size, adding or removing beads until the bracelet is the right length. Remove the bead stop. Tie the cord with a surgeon's knot *(Fig. 2)* and apply a drop of glue to the knot. Once dry, trim the cord ends.

Fig. 2

To make the Chain Bracelet:
1. Cut 3 lengths of chain the desired bracelet length, minus the length of clasp.
2. Use a jump ring *(page 95)* to attach one end of each chain to one end of the clasp.
3. Repeat Step 2, attaching the loose chain ends to the other end of the clasp.

FEATHER NECKLACE

Approx. length: 29", excluding pendant

You'll need:
- ◆ gold peacock feather pendant
- ◆ gold chain
- ◆ gold toggle clasp
- ◆ large gold jump rings
- ◆ chain-nose pliers and wire cutters

Read Jewelry Making Basics, pages 90-96, before making your necklace.

To make the necklace:
1. Attach a jump ring to the pendant *(page 95)*. Thread a 28" chain length through the jump ring.
2. Use jump rings to attach the clasp to the chain ends.

CRYSTAL EARRINGS

You'll need:
- 2 large clear acrylic beads
- 2 medium crystal beads
- 2 small gold/rhinestone beads
- 2 small blue crystal beads
- 2 silver head pins
- 2 large silver kidney ear wires with attached rhinestones
- chain-nose pliers, round-nose pliers, and wire cutters

Read Jewelry Making Basics, pages 90-96, before making your earrings.

For each earring:
1. Make a bead dangle *(page 95)* using a head pin and beads.
2. Slide the dangle on the ear wire.

PEARL & CRYSTAL NECKLACES

Long Crystal Necklace
Approx. length: 44"

You'll need:
- assorted medium and small silver, clear, and faux pearl beads (we used 202)
- beading thread
- beading needle
- jeweler's glue

Read Jewelry Making Basics, pages 90-96, before making your necklace.

To make the Long Crystal Necklace:
1. With a bead stop *(Fig. 1)* at one end, thread beads on a 56" thread length until the beaded section is 44" long.

Fig. 1

2. Remove the bead stop. Tie the ends together with a surgeon's knot *(Fig. 2)*. Place a drop of glue on the knot. When dry, trim the thread ends.

Fig. 2

Black Pendant Necklace
Approx. length: 26", excluding pendant

You'll need:
- crystal and black pendant
- large and medium faux pearls (we used 40)
- medium crystal beads (we used 41)
- small crystal beads for beaded bail (we used 15)
- silver hook and eye clasp
- silver nylon-coated beading wire
- silver crimp beads and crimp tool
- beading thread
- beading needle
- jeweler's glue
- wire cutters

Read Jewelry Making Basics, pages 90-96, before making your necklace.

To make the Black Pendant Necklace:
1. Use a crimp bead *(page 96)* to attach one clasp end to a 30" wire length. Reserving the small crystal beads for the pendant bail, thread all other beads on the wire until the beaded section is 25" long. Use a crimp bead to attach the remaining clasp end to the necklace.

2. To make the beaded pendant bail, place a bead stop on the beading thread *(Fig. 3)*. Thread the small crystal beads on the beading thread until the beaded section is 2¹/₂" long. Thread the pendant on the bail. Remove the bead stop and tie the beading thread with a surgeon's knot *(Fig. 4)*, forming a ring. Apply a drop of glue to the knot. Once dry, trim the beading thread ends.

Fig. 3

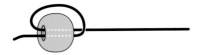

Fig. 4

3. Slide the pendant on the necklace.

Rhinestone Box Clasp Necklace
Approx. length: 18"

You'll need:
- small faux pearls (we used 50)
- small crystal beads (we used 51)
- silver/rhinestone box clasp
- silver nylon-coated beading wire
- silver crimp beads and crimp tool
- wire cutters

Read Jewelry Making Basics, pages 90-96, before making your necklace.

To make the Rhinestone Box Clasp Necklace:
1. Use a crimp bead *(page 96)* to attach one end of the clasp to a 22" wire length.
2. Thread beads on the wire until the beaded section is 17" long.
3. Use a crimp bead to attach the remaining clasp end to the necklace.

PURPLE BRACELET DUO

For the Rhinestone Clasp Bracelet, you'll need:
- large purple glass beads (we used 4)
- assorted small silver, black, and purple beads (we used 30)
- silver/rhinestone spacers (we used 3)
- silver/rhinestone box clasp
- silver nylon-coated beading wire
- silver crimp beads and crimp tool
- wire cutters

For the Stretchy Bracelet, you'll need:
- 2-hole silver/rhinestone slider beads (we used 6)
- assorted medium pink, smoke, and black crystal beads (we used 36)
- stretch cord
- jeweler's glue
- flexible wire beading needle (optional)

Read Jewelry Making Basics, pages 90-96, before making your bracelets.

To make the Rhinestone Clasp Bracelet:
1. Use a crimp bead *(page 96)* to attach one end of the clasp to a 12" wire length.
2. Thread the beads and spacers on the wire. Check the bracelet size, adding or removing beads until the bracelet is the right length.
3. Use a crimp bead to attach the remaining clasp end to the bracelet.

To make the Stretchy Bracelet:
1. With bead stops *(Fig. 1)* at the end of two 12" lengths of cord, thread the beads and sliders on cords.

Fig. 1

2. Check the bracelet size, adding or removing beads and sliders, until the bracelet is the right length. Remove the bead stops. Tie each cord with a surgeon's knot *(Fig. 2)* and apply a drop of glue to the knot. Once dry, trim the cord ends.

Fig. 2

FRINGE EARRINGS

You'll need:
- ◆ 10 assorted medium beads (in pairs)
- ◆ 2 antique gold cones
- ◆ small gold chain
- ◆ 2 gold jump rings
- ◆ 2 gold eye pins
- ◆ 2 gold ear wires
- ◆ chain-nose pliers, round-nose pliers, and wire cutters

Read Jewelry Making Basics, pages 90-96, before making your earrings.

For each earring:
1. Cut six 2$^1/_2$" chain lengths. Use a jump ring *(page 95)* to attach the chains to an eye pin.
2. Thread the eye pin through a cone. Thread beads on the eye pin. Make a loop *(page 95)* at the wire end and attach to an ear wire.

PINK PENDANT NECKLACE

Approx. length: 26", excluding pendant

You'll need:

◆ large pink acrylic gemstone bead
◆ medium and small pink acrylic beads (we used 3)
◆ assorted small silver and crystal beads and spacers (we used 9)
◆ pre-made beaded cluster (**Photo 1**)
◆ silver/rhinestone chain with rhinestone chain ends
◆ small silver chain
◆ silver lobster clasp
◆ silver jump rings
◆ silver head pins
◆ silver nylon-coated beading wire
◆ silver crimp beads and crimp tool
◆ chain-nose pliers, round-nose pliers, and wire cutters

Photo 1

Read Jewelry Making Basics, pages 90-96, before making your necklace.

To make the necklace:

1. For the pendant, thread a 12" wire length through the beaded cluster. With the cluster centered on the wire, fold the wire in half and thread the silver beads, spacers, and the gemstone bead on the wire (**Fig. 1**). Use a crimp bead *(page 96)* to attach the wire ends to the center of a 26" length of rhinestone chain.

Fig. 1

2. Make a bead dangle *(page 95)* using a head pin and a pink bead. Attach the dangle to a 1" chain length. Make 2 more bead dangles, using head pins and beads. Use jump rings *(page 95)* to attach the dangles to the pendant.
3. Attach the rhinestone chain ends to the last stone on the ends of the rhinestone chain (**Fig. 2**).

Fig. 2

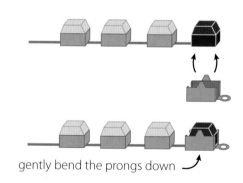

gently bend the prongs down

4. Use jump rings to attach the clasp to the rhinestone chain.

PURPLE EARRINGS

You'll need:

- 12 assorted medium and small beads and spacers (in pairs)
- 2 silver/rhinestone oval links
- 2 silver ear wires
- 2 silver head pins
- 2 silver eye pins
- chain-nose pliers, round-nose pliers, and wire cutters

Read Jewelry Making Basics, pages 90-96, before making your earrings.

For each earring:

1. Make a bead dangle *(page 95)* using a bead and a head pin. Attach the dangle to an oval link *(page 95)*.

2. To make the beaded connector, thread the beads on an eye pin. Make a loop at the wire end *(Photo 1)*.

Photo 1

3. Join the connector to the oval link and the ear wire.

SUEDE CORD MEDALLION NECKLACE

Approx. length: 36", excluding pendant

You'll need:

◆ silver/crystal/faux pearl medallion pendant with attached bail
◆ purple suede cord

Read Jewelry Making Basics, pages 90-96, before making your necklace.

To make the necklace:

1. Thread the pendant on a 40" cord length.
2. Knot the cord ends together.

PURPLE BRACELET TRIO

For the Heart Clasp Bracelet, you'll need:
- assorted medium and small purple beads and silver spacers (we used 16)
- silver/rhinestone oval links (we used 3)
- silver nylon-coated beading wire
- silver toggle clasp with heart charm
- silver crimp beads and crimp tool
- wire cutters

For the Stretchy Bracelets, you'll need:
- assorted medium and small beads (we used about 40-45 per bracelet)
- stretch cord
- jeweler's glue
- flexible wire beading needle (optional)

Read Jewelry Making Basics, pages 90-96, before making your bracelets.

To make the Heart Clasp Bracelet:
1. Use a crimp bead *(page 96)* to attach one clasp end to a 6" wire length. Thread 3 beads on the wire. Use a crimp bead to attach the wire end to an oval link *(Photo 1)*.

Photo 1

2. Continue adding beaded wire lengths and links until the bracelet is the right length, attaching the remaining clasp end to the last beaded wire length.

To make the Stretchy Bracelets:
1. For each stretchy bracelet, use a bead stop *(Fig. 1)* at one end of a 12" length of stretch cord. Thread beads on the cord.

Fig. 1

2. Check the bracelet size, adding or removing beads until bracelet is the desired length. Remove the bead stop. Tie the cord with a surgeon's knot *(Fig. 2)* and apply a drop of glue to the knot. Once dry, trim the cord ends.

Fig. 2

BLUE CAMEO NECKLACE SET

Cameo Necklace approx. length: 23", excluding pendant
Beaded Strands approx. lengths: 28" to 46"

You'll need:
- ◆ blue cameo cluster pendant with attached bail
- ◆ assorted blue seed beads
- ◆ beading thread
- ◆ beading needle
- ◆ jeweler's glue

Read Jewelry Making Basics, pages 90-96, before making your necklaces.

To make the necklace set:

1. With a bead stop on one end **(Fig. 1)**, thread beads on a 35" beading thread length until the beaded section is 23" long. Repeat to make a second beaded strand. Thread both strands through the pendant bail.

Fig. 1

2. Remove the bead stops. Tie the thread ends of each strand in a surgeon's knot **(Fig. 2)**. Add a drop of glue to knot. Once dry, trim the thread ends.

Fig. 2

3. Make 4 more beaded necklaces, varying the lengths as desired.

ILLUSION BRACELET

You'll need:

◆ medium crystal beads (we used 8 green and 8 blue)
◆ medium silver/rhinestone beads (we used 3)
◆ small silver textured beads (we used 24)
◆ small shiny silver beads (we used 4)
◆ silver seed beads (we used 12)
◆ silver nylon-coated beading wire
◆ large silver jump rings
◆ silver toggle clasp
◆ silver crimp beads and crimp tool
◆ chain-nose pliers and wire cutters

Read Jewelry Making Basics, pages 90-96, before making your bracelet.

For this bracelet, you'll need to decide the bracelet length ahead of time, taking into account the length of the clasp. Do not add bead groups past this determined length.

To make the bracelet:

1. Use crimp beads *(page 96)* to attach the centers of two 24" wire lengths to a jump ring **(Photo 1)**.

Photo 1

2. For each bead group, secure a crimp bead on a wire. Thread 3-5 beads and another crimp bead on the wire; secure the crimp bead. Continue adding bead groups, spacing them along the wires as desired **(Photo 2)**. Repeat with the remaining beads and wires.

Photo 2

3. Use crimp beads to attach the wire ends to a jump ring. Attach the clasp to the jump rings *(page 95)*.

CHARMING NECKLACE

Approx. length: 34", excluding pendant

You'll need:
◆ bronze watch face pendant with attached charms, faux pearl dangle, and rhinestone dangle
◆ 2 large leopard print flat round beads
◆ medium gold/rhinestone beads (we used 25)
◆ medium bronze beads (we used 27)
◆ gold chain in 2 sizes
◆ gold eye pins
◆ gold head pins
◆ large gold jump rings
◆ gold toggle clasp
◆ gold crimp tubes
◆ chain-nose pliers, round-nose pliers, and wire cutters

Read Jewelry Making Basics, pages 90-96, before making your necklace.

To make the necklace:

1. To make a short connector, thread 6 beads on an eye pin. Make a loop *(page 95)* at the wire end *(Photo 1)*. Repeat to make 2 long connectors using 7 beads. Join the connectors *(page 95)* to make one beaded segment *(Photo 2)*.

Photo 1

Photo 2

2. Use a jump ring to attach one end of the beaded segment to an 11½" length of the larger chain. Use a jump ring to attach the remaining end of the beaded segment to the pendant.
3. Repeat Steps 1-2 to make the other side of the necklace.
4. Make 2 bead dangles, using head pins, crimp beads, gold/rhinestone beads, and leopard print beads. Use jump rings to attach the dangles to the ends of a 4½" small chain length. Attach the chain to the pendant with a jump ring.
5. Make a long bead dangle, using a head pin and beads. Use a jump ring to attach the bead dangle to the pendant.
6. Use jump rings to attach the clasp to the necklace.

CHAPTER FOUR

rocker

Make blazing hot jewelry with cool beads, pendants, and charms!
These high-energy fashions are stunningly easy to create. Check out
the fun techniques of our jewelry making basics, starting on page 90.
From soulful hearts and crosses to impressive chains and leather cord,
you can wear and celebrate the wildly dynamic spirit of ROCK.

BLACK CHARM BRACELET

You'll need:
- large black acrylic beads (we used 11)
- black rhinestone spacers (we used 8)
- assorted charms and a bead
- silver jump rings
- silver eye pin
- stretch cord
- jeweler's glue
- chain-nose pliers, round-nose pliers, and wire cutters

Read Jewelry Making Basics, pages 90-96, before making your bracelet.

To make the bracelet:
1. With a bead stop at one end *(Fig. 1)*, thread beads and spacers on a 12" length of cord.

Fig. 1

2. Check the bracelet size, adding or removing beads and spacers until the bracelet is the right length. Remove the bead stop. Tie the cord with a surgeon's knot *(Fig. 2)* and apply a drop of glue to the knot. Once dry, trim the cord ends.

Fig. 2

3. To make the beaded connector, thread the bead on the eye pin. Make a loop *(page 95)* at the wire end *(Photo 1)*. Attach the connector to a charm *(page 95)*.

Photo 1

4. Use jump rings to attach the charms to the bracelet.

BLACK HEART NECKLACE

You'll need:

◆ pre-made braided leather necklace
◆ black heart pendant with jump ring
◆ red/silver metal link
◆ large silver jump ring
◆ chain-nose pliers

Read Jewelry Making Basics, pages 90-96, before making your necklace.

To make the necklace:
Use the jump rings *(page 95)* to attach the pendant to the metal link and the link to the necklace.

BLACK DANGLE EARRINGS

You'll need:
- ◆ 2 large black beads
- ◆ 6 medium black beads
- ◆ 20 small black beads
- ◆ tiny silver chain
- ◆ 2 silver ear wires
- ◆ silver jump rings
- ◆ silver head pins
- ◆ silver eye pins
- ◆ chain-nose pliers, round-nose pliers, and wire cutters

Read Jewelry Making Basics, pages 90-96, before making your earrings.

For each earring:
1. Make 9 single bead dangles *(page 95)*, each using a head pin and a small bead.
2. Attach a jump ring *(page 95)* to 2 single bead dangles, forming a cluster. Make 2 clusters.
3. To make the beaded connector, thread a medium bead on an eye pin. Make a loop at the wire end *(Photo 1)*. Make 3 connectors. Make another connector with a small bead on an eye pin.

Photo 1

4. For the long center dangle, join a medium bead connector to the small bead connector. Add a single bead dangle at the bottom.
5. For the two outer dangles, join a medium connector to a single bead dangle.
6. Thread a large bead on an eye pin. Make a loop at the wire end.
7. Join a length of chain to a loop on the large bead. Wrap the chain around the bead to the opposite loop and join *(Fig. 1)*; cut the excess chain. Repeat to add the chain to the bottom of the large bead.

Fig. 1

8. Attach a ⅝" long chain length and 2 single bead dangles to the ear wire. Use a jump ring to attach the chain end to the top chain on the large bead. Attach the clusters and longer dangles to the chains.

CHUNKY & CHARMING BRACELETS

For the Chunky Bracelet, you'll need:
- large red acrylic beads (we used 4)
- medium red acrylic beads (we used 5)
- small crystal beads (we used 9)
- stretch cord
- jeweler's glue
- flexible wire beading needle (optional)

For the Charming Bracelet, you'll need:
- 4 assorted large metal-lined red and black glass beads
- 4 assorted silver metal spacer beads
- 5 red and black jeweled spacer beads
- small black chain
- tiny rhinestone chain with rhinestone chain ends
- silver jump rings
- silver toggle clasp
- chain-nose pliers and wire cutters

Read Jewelry Making Basics, pages 90-96, before making your bracelets.

To make the Chunky Bracelet:
1. With a bead stop at one end, thread beads on a 12" length of cord *(Fig. 1)*.

Fig. 1

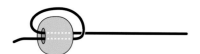

2. Check the bracelet size, adding or removing beads until the bracelet is the right length. Remove the stop bead. Tie the cord with a surgeon's knot *(Fig. 2)* and apply a drop of glue to the knot. Once dry, trim the cord ends.

Fig. 2

To make the Charming Bracelet:
1. Cut a length of each chain the desired bracelet length, minus the length of the clasp. Attach a rhinestone chain end to the last stone on each end of the rhinestone chain *(Fig. 3)*.

Fig. 3

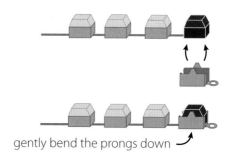

gently bend the prongs down

2. Use a jump ring *(page 95)* to attach both chains to the bar of the clasp. Thread the beads and spacers on the chains.
3. Use a jump ring to attach the remaining clasp end to the chains.

CAMEO NECKLACES

Approx. length: 24" each, excluding pendant

For the Cameo Necklace, you'll need:
- cameo pendant (we colored the background with a black permanent marker)
- long silver bugle beads (we used 32)
- small crystal beads (we used 34)
- medium crystal beads (we used 16)
- silver nylon-coated beading wire
- silver S-hook clasp
- silver jump rings
- silver crimp beads and crimp tool
- chain-nose pliers and wire cutters

For the Chain Necklace, you'll need:
- black chain
- black toggle clasp
- black jump rings
- chain-nose pliers and wire cutters

Read Jewelry Making Basics, pages 90-96, before making your necklaces.

To make the Cameo Necklace:
1. Use a crimp bead *(page 96)* to attach a jump ring to a 28" wire length. Thread beads on the wire until the beaded section is 24" long. Use a crimp bead to attach the ring part of the clasp.
2. Use the jump ring *(page 95)* on the beaded section to attach the hook part of the clasp.
3. Use a jump ring to attach the pendant to the necklace.

To make the Chain Necklace:
1. Cut a 23" chain length.
2. Use jump rings *(page 95)* to attach the clasp to the chain ends.

CHAIN & LEATHER NECKLACE

Approx. length: 20", excluding pendant

You'll need:

◆ wings pendant with attached interchangeable bail **(Photo 1)**
◆ key ring for large metal-lined glass beads **(Photo 2)**
◆ assorted large black, clear, and silver beads
◆ red jeweled spacer bead
◆ silver chain
◆ black ribbon
◆ black leather cord
◆ 2 cord ends
◆ silver jump rings
◆ chain-nose pliers and wire cutters

Read Jewelry Making Basics, pages 90-96, before making your necklace.

Photo 1

Photo 2

To make the necklace:

1. Thread the ribbon through the links of an 11" chain length. Use the chain-nose pliers to attach the cord ends to the ribbon. Use jump rings *(page 95)* to attach the cord ends to the chain ends.
2. Fold a 15" leather cord length in half and knot through a chain end. Repeat for the remaining chain end. Knot the leather cord ends together.

3. Take the pendant apart to use the wings and the bail. Take the key chain apart to use the bead pin.
4. Unscrew the bead pin top. Thread the spacer and beads on the pin and replace the top. Use a jump ring to attach the bead pin to the wings. Use the bail to attach the pendant to the chain center.

CROSS PENDANT NECKLACE

Approx. length: 18", excluding pendant

You'll need:
- ◆ cross pendant
- ◆ medium clear beads (we used 80)
- ◆ medium red beads (we used 80)
- ◆ medium black beads (we used 12)
- ◆ black seed beads (we used 152)
- ◆ large silver jump rings
- ◆ silver nylon-coated beading wire
- ◆ silver clasp with extension chain
- ◆ silver crimp beads and crimp tool
- ◆ chain-nose pliers and wire cutters
- ◆ beading thread
- ◆ beading needle
- ◆ jeweler's glue

Read Jewelry Making Basics, pages 90-96, before making your necklace.

To make the necklace:
1. Use a crimp bead *(page 96)* to attach a jump ring *(page 95)* to a 22" wire length. Thread the clear beads on the wire until the beaded section is 17" long. Use a crimp bead to attach another jump ring.
2. Use a crimp bead to attach a 22" wire length to the jump ring on the clear beaded strand. Thread the red beads on the wire until the beaded section is 17" long. Use a crimp bead to attach the red beaded strand to the remaining jump ring on the clear strand.
3. Repeat Step 2 with the black beads.
4. Use the jump rings to attach the strands to the clasp.

5. To make the beaded pendant bail, place a bead stop on the beading thread *(Fig. 1)*. Thread the seed beads on the beading thread until the beaded section is 2½" long. Remove the bead stop. Tie the thread with a surgeon's knot *(Fig. 2)*, forming a ring. Apply a drop of glue to the knot. Once dry, trim the thread ends.

Fig. 1

Fig. 2

6. Attach the pendant to the beaded bail with a jump ring. Slide the pendant on the necklace.

HEARTS PENDANT NECKLACE

Approx. length: 33", excluding pendant

You'll need:
- antique silver/red hearts pendant with attached bail
- black chain
- 21" length leopard print ribbon
- black toggle clasp
- black jump rings
- chain-nose pliers and wire cutters
- fabric glue

Read Jewelry Making Basics, pages 90-96, before making your necklace.

To make the necklace:
1. Cut two 8" lengths of chain. Use jump rings *(page 95)* to attach the clasp to one end of each chain.
2. Thread the pendant to the center of the ribbon. Tie an overhand knot near the pendant. Thread each ribbon end through a chain end. Fold and glue the ribbon to the wrong side.

HOOP EARRINGS

You'll need:

◆ 2 silver hoop earrings
◆ 14 assorted small beads and charms (in pairs)
◆ silver jump rings
◆ silver head pins
◆ silver eye pins
◆ chain-nose pliers, round-nose pliers, and wire cutters

Read Jewelry Making Basics, pages 90-96, before making your earrings.

For each earring:

1. To make the beaded connector, thread 3 beads on an eye pin. Make a loop *(page 95)* at the wire end **(Photo 1)**. Use a jump ring *(page 95)* to attach a charm to the connector bottom. Attach a jump ring to the connector top.

Photo 1

2. Make a bead dangle using a head pin and a bead. Attach a jump ring to the dangle.
3. Thread the connector, charms, and bead dangle on the hoop earring, adding jump rings if necessary for the charms to hang straight.

KEY PENDANT NECKLACE

Approx. length: 32", excluding pendant

You'll need:
- ◆ key pendant for large metal-lined glass beads
- ◆ 2 assorted large metal-lined black glass beads
- ◆ 2 red and black jeweled spacer beads
- ◆ large silver jump ring
- ◆ 1 yd red ribbon
- ◆ chain-nose pliers

Read Jewelry Making Basics, pages 90-96, before making your necklace.

To make the necklace:
1. Unscrew the top of the key pendant. Thread the beads and spacers on the pendant and replace the top.
2. Attach a jump ring *(page 95)* to the pendant and thread on the ribbon. Knot the ribbon ends together.

STRETCHY BRACELETS

For each bracelet, you'll need:
- ◆ assorted medium and small glass and metal beads (about 27-50 per bracelet)
- ◆ stretch cord
- ◆ jeweler's glue
- ◆ flexible wire beading needle (optional)

You'll also need:
- ◆ ribbon

Read Jewelry Making Basics, pages 90-96, before making your bracelets.

To make each bracelet:
1. With a bead stop at one end, thread beads on a 12" length of cord *(Fig. 1)*.

Fig. 1

2. Check the bracelet size, adding or removing beads until the bracelet is the right length. Remove the bead stop. Tie the cord with a surgeon's knot *(Fig. 2)* and apply a drop of glue to the knot. Once dry, trim the cord ends.

Fig. 2

3. Make 4 bracelets. Tie 3 together with ribbon.

TASSEL EARRINGS

You'll need:
- 2 rhinestone charms
- 2 large clear acrylic beads
- 4 small red beads
- 2 small silver beads
- 2 red/silver metal links
- small black chain
- 2 large silver kidney ear wires
- silver eye pins
- silver jump rings
- chain-nose pliers, round-nose pliers, and wire cutters

Read Jewelry Making Basics, pages 90-96, before making your earrings.

For each earring:
1. To make the beaded connector, thread the beads on an eye pin. Make a loop *(page 95)* at the wire end **(Photo 1)**. Attach the rhinestone charm to the connector bottom *(page 95)*.

Photo 1

2. Cut 6 lengths of chain, varying the lengths from 2" to 3¹/₂". Use a jump ring to attach the chains to a metal link. Use another jump ring to attach the connector to the link.
3. Slide the link on the ear wire.

WINGS CHARM BRACELET

You'll need:

- assorted medium and small red, silver, and clear beads (we used 71)
- assorted silver wing charms (we used 7)
- silver chain bracelet
- silver nylon-coated beading wire
- large silver jump rings
- silver crimp beads and crimp tool
- chain-nose pliers and wire cutters

Read Jewelry Making Basics, pages 90-96, before making your bracelet.

To make the bracelet:

1. Use a crimp bead *(page 96)* to attach a jump ring to a 14" wire length. Thread beads on the wire until the beaded section is the same length as the chain link section of the bracelet. Use a crimp bead to attach a jump ring at the end.
2. Repeat Step 1 to make another beaded strand.
3. Use the end jump rings *(page 95)* to attach the beaded strands to the bracelet clasp.
4. Use jump rings to attach the charms to the bracelet links.

CHARM CHOKER

Approx. length: 16", excluding charms

Photo 1   **Photo 2**

You'll need:
♦ assorted large and medium red and black beads (we used 37)
♦ assorted silver and black charms (we used 12)
♦ antique silver chain
♦ antique silver jump rings
♦ antique silver head pins and eye pins
♦ antique silver toggle clasp
♦ chain-nose pliers, round-nose pliers, and wire cutters

Read Jewelry Making Basics, pages 90-96, before making your choker.

To make the choker:
1. Make 19 bead dangles *(page 95)* using head pins and 1-3 beads.
2. To make the beaded connector, thread a bead on an eye pin. Make a loop at the wire end **(Photo 1)**. Make 6 connectors. Use a jump ring *(page 95)* to attach a charm to each connector **(Photo 2)**.
3. Use jump rings to attach dangles, connectors, and charms to the center 5" of a 15" chain length.
4. Use jump rings to attach the clasp to the chain ends.

SPARKLE BRACELETS

For Heart Bracelet, you'll need:
- small cracked glass beads (we used 5)
- medium cracked glass beads (we used 6)
- silver bead caps (2 for each medium bead)
- silver/rhinestone heart pendant
- large silver jump ring
- stretch cord
- jeweler's glue
- chain-nose pliers
- flexible wire beading needle (optional)

For Chain Bracelet, you'll need:
- small black beads (we used 16)
- rhinestone chain with rhinestone chain ends
- pre-made black leather bracelet
- silver chain
- silver nylon-coated beading wire
- large silver jump rings
- silver crimp beads and crimp tool
- chain-nose pliers and wire cutters

Read Jewelry Making Basics, pages 90-96, before making your bracelets.

To make Heart Bracelet:
1. With a bead stop at one end *(Fig. 1)*, thread beads and bead caps on a 12" length of cord.

Fig. 1

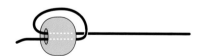

2. Check the bracelet size, adding or removing beads until the bracelet is the right length. Remove the bead stop. Tie the cord with a surgeon's knot *(Fig. 2)* and apply a drop of glue to the knot. Once dry, trim the cord ends.

Fig. 2

3. Use the jump ring *(page 95)* to attach the pendant to the bracelet.

To make Chain Bracelet:
1. For the beaded section, use a crimp bead *(page 96)* to attach a jump ring to an 8" wire length. Thread beads on the wire until the beaded section is 4" long. Use a crimp bead to attach another jump ring.
2. Attach a rhinestone chain end to the last stone on each end of two 4¹/₂" lengths of rhinestone chain *(Fig. 3)*.

Fig. 3

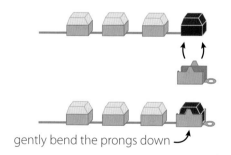

gently bend the prongs down

3. Cut a piece of chain the same length as the leather bracelet. Thread the leather bracelet through the chain near the ends. Attach the chain to the bracelet jump rings *(page 95)*.

4. Use jump rings to attach the beaded section and the rhinestone chains to the silver chain.

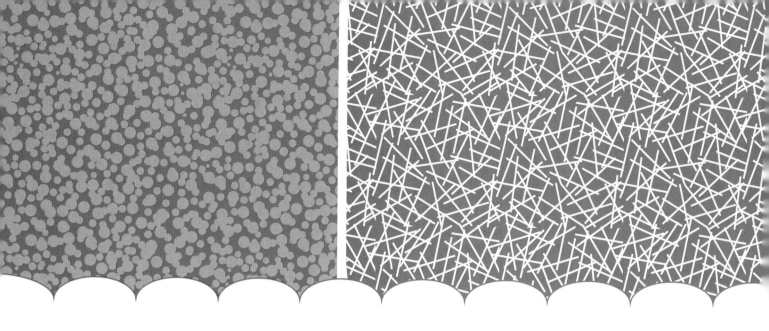

JEWELRY MAKING BASICS

Sizing It Up

This table and drawing show various necklace lengths and about where they fall on the body. The lengths are commonly used in the jewelry world, but feel free to adjust your necklaces to suit you and your fashion sense.

Common Jewelry Lengths

Bracelet	6" to 8"
Choker	14" to 16"
Princess	17" to 19"
Matinee	20" to 24"
Opera	28" to 34"
Rope	40" to 45"
Lariat	Over 45"

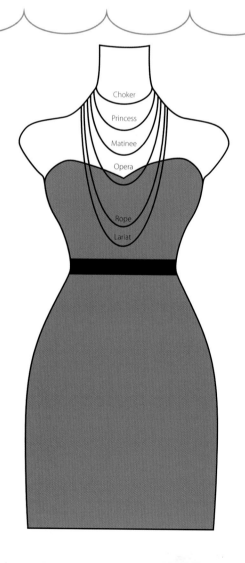

CHOOSING BEADS

Beads come in all sizes, shapes, colors, finishes, and materials.

Ceramic and stone beads come in several shapes and may be glazed or similarly textured.

Plastic or acrylic beads are lightweight and can give a more whimsical look to your jewelry. Some metal-look beads are plastic; others may be highly polished to look like glass.

Crystal beads have multiple machine-cut facets that capture and reflect light with lots of sparkle. They come in dozens of colors, sizes, and shapes.

Seed beads are usually the smallest beads and are available in different sizes, shapes, and colors. This category includes small round beads, small tube beads, bugle beads, and the larger e-beads.

Faux pearls have a synthetic coating over a crystal, glass, or plastic base. They are very uniform in size, shape, and color.

Shell beads have a lustrous finish. They can be uniform in size, shape, and color or be more varied and organic. They can even be actual whole shells!

Glass beads come in all sizes, shapes, and colors. Some have a shiny, polished, or iridescent finish, while others may have a matte finish.

Wood beads give your jewelry a natural, organic look. They are available in many sizes, shapes, and finishes.

Metal beads, including spacers and spacer beads, can be made of base metal (which is nonprecious) or plated metals.

CHOOSING FINDINGS

Findings are the components used to assemble jewelry.

Beading thread is strong and has very little stretch. This soft thread easily passes through a beading needle's eye, knots well, and will create a soft, flowing jewelry piece.

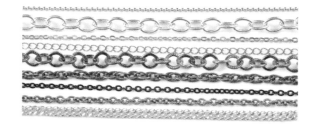

Chains come in a variety of sizes, styles, colors, and finishes.

Leather and suede cords come in a variety of sizes and colors and are used for a more casual look.

Nylon-coated beading wire is made up of multiple strands of metal that are twisted together and coated with nylon; the more strands, the stronger and more flexible the wire. It is available in various diameters and strengths.

Stretch cord is great for bracelets and is more durable than thin elastic. A drop of jeweler's glue on the knot will keep the bracelet secure.

Cord is available in many colors and may be cotton, linen, or jute.

Bead caps add texture and sparkle when placed next to beads.

Clasps of all sizes, shapes, and styles are available. Lobster clasps are shaped like a lobster's claw and have a spring-action closure. A toggle clasp is secured by sliding the bar through the loop. There are also spring-ring clasps, hook and eye clasps, box clasps, and magnetic clasps.

Cones are findings that hide the ends of multi-strand jewelry pieces.

Cord ends fit over the ends of ribbon, leather, and cord. They may be crimped and/or glued in place.

Crimp beads or tubes are small metal beads that are flattened over jewelry wire to finish the ends or hold elements in place. The beads are rounded and the tubes are cylinder-shaped. Both come in many sizes and finishes.

Just about any earring style can be made with the wide variety of **ear wires** available–large kidney, fishhook, hoop, pinch bail, etc.

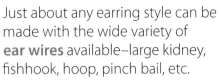

Head pins & eye pins are very similar and are used in similar situations when making jewelry. A head pin is a straight wire with a head of some sort; many are flat, but there are several decorative styles as well. An eye pin is also a straight wire, but it has a loop at one end. This loop may be opened and closed with chain-nose pliers, just like a jump ring.

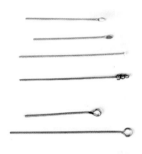

Jump rings are metal rounds or ovals that are used to attach jewelry components to each other. The rings are opened and closed with chain-nose pliers.

Spacer bars keep beaded strands separate on bracelets and necklaces. Some are very decorative and become a design element, while others are more discreet in their appearance.

TOOLS & HOW TO USE THEM

The two most common types of **beading needles** are the flexible wire needle and the rigid metal needle. The eye of the flexible wire needle collapses on itself, making it easier to go through small-hole beads.

Bead mats are made of foam-like material and keep the beads from rolling all over the work surface.

Bead boards are very handy. Not only can you see your necklace or bracelet in its final arrangement, the board also has measurements so that you no longer have to guess how many beads you'll need for a specific length.

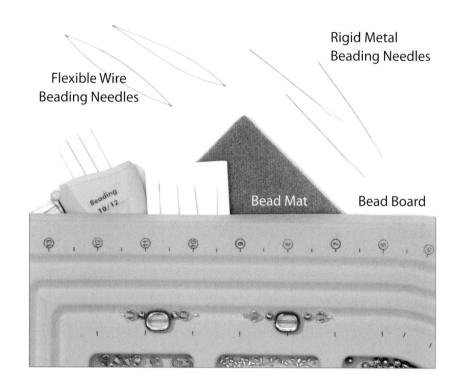

Flexible Wire Beading Needles

Rigid Metal Beading Needles

Bead Mat

Bead Board

Chain-nose pliers have rounded, tapered jaws and a flat interior surface that will not mar wire or metal findings. These pliers are used for opening and closing jump rings and bending wire. They may also be called needle-nose pliers. You'll need 2 pair to open jump rings and loops on head pins and eye pins.

Round-nose pliers have round jaws that are useful for making loops and bending wire smoothly.

Wire cutters are used to cut beading wire, head pins, eye pins, and other soft metals.

A **crimp tool** (also known as crimping pliers) flattens and shapes the crimp bead or crimp tube.

Spring bead stops keep beads from sliding off when threading beads on beading wire. Just squeeze the ends and slip the wire between the spring coils.

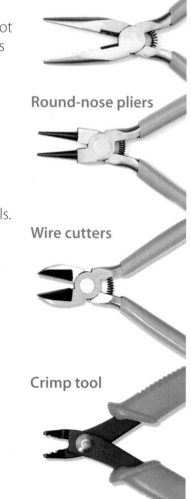

Chain-nose pliers

Round-nose pliers

Wire cutters

Crimp tool

Spring bead stops

BASIC TECHNIQUES

Using a Bead Stop

When threading beads on a thread or cord, you don't want to be concerned that the beads will slide off the other end. A bead stop does just that: it stops the beads from sliding off your beading thread.

You can simply use a larger, different colored bead. Before you start threading on your beads, thread on a bead stop. Run the beading thread or cord around the bead and pass through the bead again, securing it in place *(Fig. 1)*.

Fig. 1

When you are ready to knot the ends, loosen the thread or cord and carefully remove the bead stop. You can now tie a surgeon's knot *(page 96)*.

Making Bead Dangles on Head Pins

Slide your beads on a head pin. Leaving about $\frac{1}{2}$", cut off the excess wire. If you are making a large loop, leave more wire at the end.

Using the chain-nose pliers, bend the wire at a 90° angle *(Fig. 2)*. Grasp the wire end with the round-nose pliers. Turn the pliers and bend the wire into a loop *(Figs. 3-4)*. Release the pliers. Straighten or twist the loop further if necessary.

Loops may also be made on eye pins the same way.

Fig. 2   **Fig. 3**   **Fig. 4**

       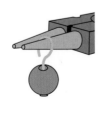

Opening and Closing Jump Rings and Loops on Head Pins or Eye Pins

Whether you need to attach a clasp, charm, dangle, or other jewelry component, you'll probably use jump rings. Here's how to properly open and close them.

Pick up a jump ring with chain-nose pliers. With a second pair of chain-nose pliers, gently hold the other side of the ring. Open the ring by pulling one pair of pliers toward you while pushing the other away *(Fig. 5)*.

Fig. 5

Close the ring by pushing and pulling the pliers in the opposite direction, bringing the ring ends back together.

You'll also open and close the loops on head pins and eye pins the same way.

Using Crimp Beads Or Tubes

To finish a wire end, thread a crimp bead or tube and the clasp or jump ring on the wire. Run the wire back through the crimp bead; use a pair of pliers to pull and tighten the wire *(Fig. 6)*. Place the crimp bead or tube on the inner groove of the crimp tool and squeeze *(Fig. 7)*.

Release the tool, turn the crimp bead or tube a quarter turn, and place it in the outer groove *(Fig. 8)*. Squeeze the tool to round out the crimp bead or tube *(Fig. 9)*. Trim the wire end or if the design calls for beads, thread the beads over the wire to cover the end.

Tying Knots

Tie an **overhand knot** with cords, suede cords, or ribbon *(Fig. 10)*.

Fig. 10

Tie a **surgeon's knot** *(Fig. 11)* when using stretch cord or beading thread. Add a drop of jeweler's glue to the knot for extra strength.

Fig. 11

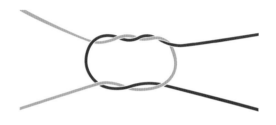

Fig. 6

Fig. 7

Fig. 8

Fig. 9